Copyright © 2019 by Tim Dimmick

All rights reserved. No part of this publication may be reproduced, distributed or transmitted in any form or by any means, without prior written permission.

Ask Tim Dimmick. -- 1st ed.
ISBN 978-1-0951669-4-9

The Publisher has strived to be as accurate and complete as possible in the creation of this book.

This book is not intended for use as a source of legal, business, accounting or financial advice. All readers are advised to seek services of competent professionals in legal, business, accounting, and finance field.

In practical advice books, like anything else in life, there are no guarantees of income or results made. Readers are cautioned to rely on their own judgment about their individual circumstances to act accordingly.

While all attempts have been made to verify information provided in this publication, the Publisher assumes no responsibility for errors, omissions, or contrary interpretation of the subject matter herein. Any perceived slights of specific persons, peoples, or organizations are unintentional.

Table of Contents

Introduction 1

What is a No Money Down Home Loan? 7

Should I consider buying a home with no money down even if I have $5,000 or $10,000 saved? 9

Which program actually has a 100% mortgage? 11

What if my house doesn't qualify for a USDA loan? 13

What is a Down Payment Assistance Program? 17

What is a Grant Program? 19

What Qualifies as Gifted Funds? 21

What are Closing Costs? 23

What are Lender Fees? 25

What is PMI? 27

What is Title Insurance?.............................. 29

What kind of taxes will I have to pay at closing?.. 31

How can I fund closing costs without using my savings?.. 33

Why would a seller be willing to pay my Closing Costs?... 35

What is Earnest Money?............................... 37

Are there any other upfront costs?........... 39

Will I get the upfront payments back if the deal falls through?................................ 43

Can you share an example of how you help overcome these challenges?....... 45

Should I get approved for a loan before I start house shopping?................................. 53

What's the difference between Pre-Qualification and Pre-Approval?.................. 57

What are the main things lenders are looking at when pre-approving a buyer?... 59

What makes up your credit score?............ 63

Don't I need perfect credit to qualify
for a No Money Down Mortgage? 69

Will I have to pay a higher interest
rate for a No Money Down Mortgage? 71

Can I qualify for a No Money Down
Mortgage if I already have monthly car
payments and other bills? 73

How Much Can I Be Approved For? 75

I just got a new job. Can I still qualify
for a No Money Down Mortgage? 79

Are there any pitfalls I should look out
for? 81

How much do real estate agents
charge to help me through the process
of finding the right house? 83

What inspired you to help people buy
their first home with no money down? 85

What big lesson have you learned from
working with first-time homebuyers? 89

What's the most important question
a first-time home buyer should ask
themselves before buying a home with
no money down? 91

What is the most important thing a first-time home buyer should consider when evaluating a real estate agent?........... 93

How do I get this process started?............. 95

Do you have a question for Tim?................ 97

About Tim Dimmick... 99

What Tim's Clients Are Saying.................. 101

Introduction

One of the biggest myths of home ownership is that you can't buy a home with less than 10-20% down.

In 2017, NerdWallet conducted a poll with 2000 individuals of which 33% of those polled still believe they need 20% down to buy a house. I run into that daily.

I talk to many want-to-be home buyers that are struggling to save money and don't see the light at the end of the tunnel.

A lot of young couples, especially those with young children, for one reason or another believe it's not realistic to be able to buy a house. In many cases, instead of taking the time to meet with someone who is really educated in the subject, they listen to someone giving them false information and end up renting instead.

PA NO MONEY DOWN HOMES

My focus on helping people buy a home with No Money Down came from my background in the mortgage business which gave me an understanding of the many products that exist. Most people aren't aware of these programs because of limited advertising, and the programs are not pushed by the lenders.

I educate buyers about the available programs that allow them to buy a home with little to no money down.

Many people believe a large down payment is required to buy a home. I always tell people, if you have enough money to rent a house, then you have enough money to buy a house – provided you have the required credit and income to support the payment.

When you consider today's income levels for the young home buyer who is just getting out of school with student loans, car payments, and normal living expenses, it can take a first-time home buyer a significant amount of time to save for a 5% or more down payment.

ASK TIM DIMMICK

Over the past year or two, interest rates have climbed from 3.5% to as high as 5%. So, if you are trying to save 5% or 10% for a down payment, you went backwards in the last 12 months because you're not saving money fast enough to outpace the difference that the increased interest rate is making to your payment.

In addition to an increasing rate environment, you may also be fighting the appreciation of home values in a good economy.

The combination of these two things alone can force one out of the market in terms of affordability while they are trying to save the down payment

I help my clients buy a home with a payment comparable to what they would expect to pay in rent for that same property.

Home ownership is a big deal if you've only ever rented a house in your lifetime.

PA NO MONEY DOWN HOMES

People take pride in a home when it's their own — painting, remodeling and decorating as they wish making it their own.

Home ownership plays a major role in your financial security. In addition to knowing your housing costs into the future, you're building equity with each payment you make.

Being a homeowner provides stability for you and your family because you're now in charge of where you live and how long you can live there.

It was important to me to own a home, giving my family a place to call our own.

While home ownership comes with additional responsibilities, most people are willing to take those on as a tradeoff for the security it provides for their family.

If that sounds like you, then keep reading. I'm confident this book will answer a lot of questions and help you see that your dream of becoming a homeowner is closer than you may think.

PA NO MONEY DOWN HOMES

267-217-2856

PANoMoneyDownHomes.com

PA License # RS337966

What is a No Money Down Home Loan?

A no money down home loan gives eligible first-time home buyers the opportunity to buy a property by providing financing for 100% of the purchase price for qualified homes.

Not all borrowers or houses qualify for these special loans, but there are other options out there which can achieve the same results by taking advantage of special down payment assistance programs, grants and alternative funding sources available to many first-time homebuyers.

These special financing programs are only available through lenders approved by the government agencies that back these loans by reducing the risk to lenders by guaranteeing 90% of the loan.

These programs have been around for years but are rarely talked about or completely ignored by most mortgage companies.

That's why it's important to work with real estate professionals who understand the ins and outs of these programs and how they apply to your specific situation.

> **Should I consider buying a home with no money down even if I have $5,000 or $10,000 saved?**

Absolutely. Utilizing a program to buy with no money down can provide more flexibility by using this money for closing costs or reserve savings after settlement.

I'm a big believer in having three to six months of your income stuck away for a rainy day. When I bought my first house, did I? No. But since then, I've learned how the wheels of life turn and things happen, and when they do it's nice to have some backup savings.

I certainly don't want anyone to go broke to buy a house. I don't think that's smart. I tell my clients to buy a house that's within your means.

Everybody wants a home with all the bells and whistles, and a nice kitchen with granite countertops.

The reality is there's more to life than making a mortgage payment, so keep it within your means. Banks use debt ratios and qualification ratios for a reason.

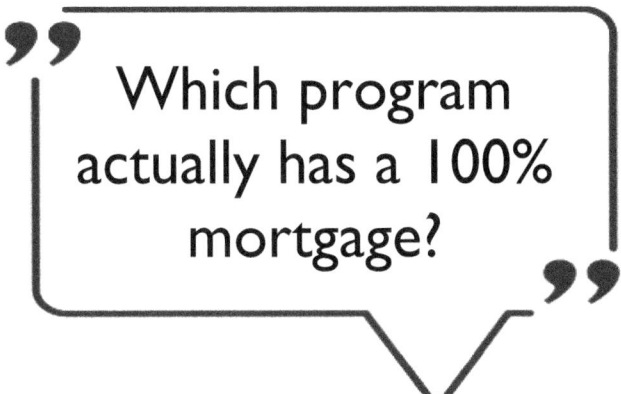
Which program actually has a 100% mortgage?

The USDA No Down Payment program has allowed me to help several families reach their dream of home ownership.

USDA?

Aren't they the ones who grade my beef?

Backed by the U.S. Department of Agriculture, the USDA Rural Housing Mortgage was created to help build up rural areas by making 100% financing available to eligible borrowers.

The USDA program is the absolute number one program that I use.

Even though this program is limited to "rural" areas, don't be deterred. I know from experience; the term is applied much more loosely than what you might expect.

While the program doesn't work in the heart of the city, I've helped many families purchase nice homes in less populated areas. Don't worry; you won't need to play a guessing game and wonder if a house you are interested in qualifies.

I send all my clients an online tool that allows them to enter an address that instantly lets them know if the house is eligible for USDA financing.

> **What if my house doesn't qualify for a USDA loan?**

If your dream house is outside of a USDA-qualified area, we can use FHA – A Low Down Payment Loan to possibly create a No Money Down scenario.

An FHA loan is a mortgage insured by the Federal Housing Administration (FHA).

While there are a few First Time Buyer programs that require as little as 3% down, an FHA loan is next in line if a house I'm working on doesn't qualify for USDA financing because these loans don't require the "rural" designation eligibility requirement.

FHA financing requires a 3.5% down payment. When a mortgage lender requires a down payment, the borrower is required to pay a certain percentage of the home's purchase price upfront.

If the purchase price of your home is $100,000, you would be able to finance $96,500 with an FHA Loan. That means you would need to have $3,500 available for a down payment.

Keep in mind that the down payment is based strictly on a percentage of the purchase price of the home. It does not include closing costs.

To break it down, USDA is a true No Down Payment Loan that will finance 100% of the borrower's purchase price. An FHA Loan requires a 3.5% down payment.

The good news is the money required for the down payment of an FHA loan can be funded through sources other than the borrower's savings. Using a down payment assistance program, grant programs or gifted funds can allow us to create a No Money Down scenario.

PA NO MONEY DOWN HOMES

267-217-2856

PANoMoneyDownHomes.com

PA License # RS337966

What is a Down Payment Assistance Program?

In Pennsylvania, we have the *PHFA Keystone Advantage Assistance Program*. The Pennsylvania Housing Finance Agency (PHFA) offers a no-interest loan program that will lend up to 4% (with a cap of $6,000) of the purchase price for qualified borrowers to use for down payment and/or closing costs.

This creates a 10-year second mortgage on your home. At 0% interest, if you borrowed the maximum of $6,000, it would only add $50 a month to your payment for the first 10 years of your mortgage.

PA NO MONEY DOWN HOMES

Keep in mind, with the $6,000 maximum, your purchase price would need to be about $170,000 for this program to cover a 3.5% down payment on an FHA Loan, creating a NO MONEY DOWN purchase option.

There are of course credit requirements and income limits, but many first-time buyers can typically qualify.

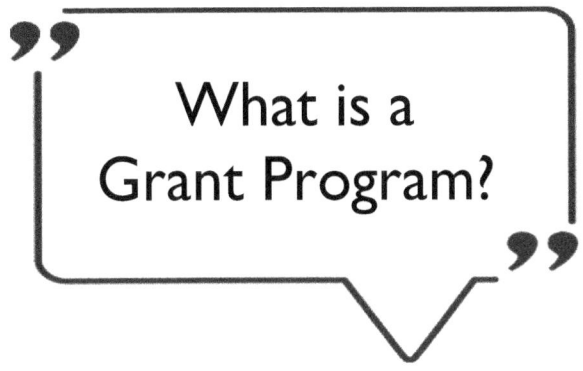

What is a Grant Program?

Grant programs are widely accepted by mortgage lenders to cover down payment and/ or closing costs.

For example, some programs will allow a homebuyer to borrow from $5000 all the way up to $10,000.

In many cases, these funds do not need to be paid back provided you live in the home for a minimum amount of time.

The details and qualifications vary by program and most grant programs are specific to the area in which you currently live or wish to purchase a home.

Once the allocated funds for a particular grant program have been disbursed the program is unavailable until the fund is replenished the next fiscal year.

Most grant programs require homebuyers to apply prior to entering into a sales contract for a house.

Typically, a prospective homebuyer needs to attend a homebuyer course for the program before receiving a certificate of qualification.

While most any mortgage loan will allow gifted funds to be applied to the down payment and/or closing costs for purchasing a home, there can be limitations on the amount based on the loan program.

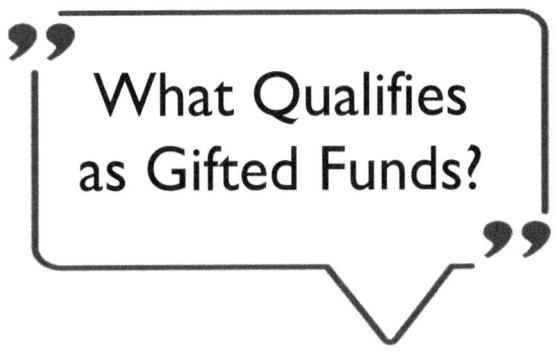

What Qualifies as Gifted Funds?

FHA Loans allow for the entire down payment to be a gift to the borrower. There are some restrictions, however.

Typically, the funds must be a gift from a parent or close relative. The gifted funds must also be documented in a "Gift Letter," which includes the relationship of the person making the gift, where the money came from, and that the funds are indeed a gift and not a loan.

While most any mortgage loan will allow gifted funds to be applied to the down payment and/or closing costs for purchasing a home, there can be limitations on the amount based on the loan program.

PA NO MONEY DOWN HOMES

267-217-2856

PANoMoneyDownHomes.com

PA License # RS337966

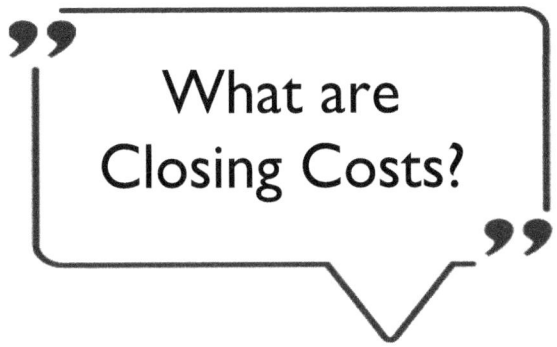

What are Closing Costs?

One area that is often misunderstood is the difference between a down payment and closing costs. Some prospective home-buyers think no money down means they can walk in, sign papers, and leave with the keys.

When buying any home, there are costs involved in the acquisition in addition to the purchase price of the home. These are called closing costs and are a completely separate expense from the down payment.

Some common closing costs you can expect when it comes to buying a house are Lenders Fees, Title Insurance and Taxes.

These can add up quickly. I tell my clients to use a general rule of thumb of 5-6% of the purchase price when estimating closing costs. So, if you are purchasing a $200,000 you can expect your closing costs to be $10,000 to $12,0000.

Like a lot of people, you may be wondering, "How is this No Money Down if it's costing me $10,000"?

Remember, a "No Down Payment" home loan only covers the purchase price of the house. However, there are ways we can fund these closing costs to make this into a true No Money Out of Pocket deal.

This is why it's important to work with a real estate professional who can assess your situation and explain the options available.

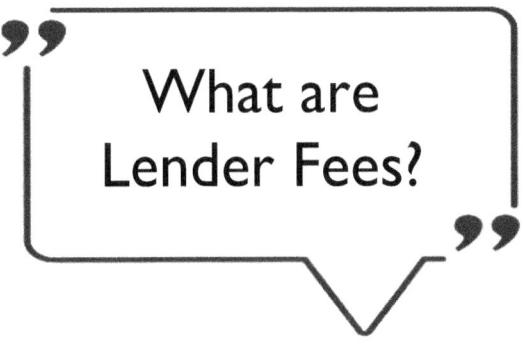

What are Lender Fees?

Lenders generally charge various fees associated with completing your loan.

These fees are separate from the purchase price of your home.

Common fees you can expect to see from a mortgage company include running your credit, underwriting and document preparation fees, and wire transfer fees. These fees typically range from $700 to $1200.

PA NO MONEY DOWN HOMES

267-217-2856

PANoMoneyDownHomes.com

PA License # RS337966

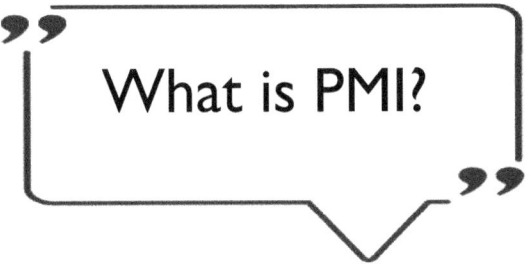

What is PMI?

Unless a borrower is making a down payment of at least 20% of the purchase price of the house, the lender will require the borrower to purchase Private Mortgage Insurance (PMI).

Private Mortgage Insurance (PMI) protects the lender in case the borrower defaults on the loan and the market value of the home is less than outstanding balance owed.

PMI rates vary based on the loan program you are using to finance the home. Some loan programs allow a borrower to pay one up front PMI premium, some will have a monthly premium, and some loan programs will have a combination of the two. The given PMI premiums will be calculated based on the program you are using to finance the home and be part of your closing costs, and/or monthly mortgage payment.

On conventional loan programs once you pay down 20% of the loan principal, you can contact the lender and request that the PMI be removed.

What is Title Insurance?

You will most likely close the purchase of your house at the office of a Title Company.

The Title Company works closely with the real estate agents and the mortgage company to calculate the final costs, handle the transaction paperwork and facilitates the transfer of funds required to complete the sale of the property.

Part of your closing costs will be to purchase Title Insurance, which protects you and the lender from any prior claims against the property.

The title company researches property's history and makes sure that there are no prior liens such as back taxes or perhaps a construction company that may have repaired the roof for the previous owner and wasn't paid.

The title company then issues a title policy that guarantees that any prior claims and liens have been satisfied.

The cost of title insurance is based on the purchase price of the property and the type of coverage you select over those required by the bank.

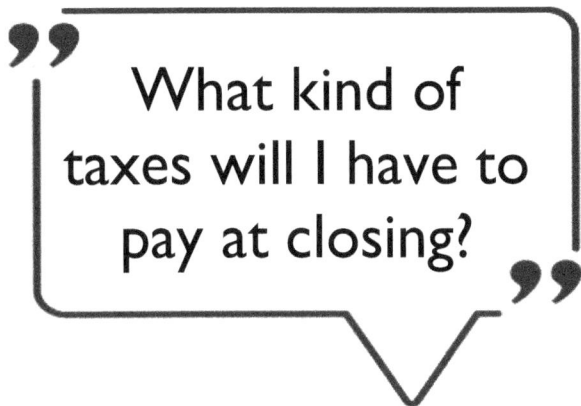

In Pennsylvania, there's a 2% transfer tax incurred every time a piece of real estate sold.

Collected by the title company at closing, this cost is typically split between the buyer and the seller, each paying 1%.

There are also property taxes. Pennsylvania real estate taxes are paid in advance. So regardless of what time of year you purchase your house, at closing the title company will collect a full year of taxes from the buyer.

A portion will reimburse the seller for any taxes that they've already prepaid for the current year and rest will be put into your mortgage escrow account which the lender will use towards paying the upcoming year's tax bill.

Pennsylvania property tax rates vary by county with the average effective property tax rate being 1.55%.

> How can I fund closing costs without using my savings?

Most of the options we talked about for funding your down payment, (Down Payment Assistance, Grant Programs, and Gifted Funds) can also be used towards closing costs, but they may not be able to cover it all.

This is where your real estate agent's negotiating and deal structuring skills can make a significant impact on how much money you need to purchase your new home by using Seller Assistance.

Most government loans like FHA typically will allow the seller to contribute up to 6%

of the buyer's closing costs. This is pretty convenient considering the 5-6% closing cost rule of thumb we talked about earlier, wouldn't you say?

The seller can only pay up to 6% of the actual closing costs. If the closing costs are only 5%, the seller would be limited to paying just that 5%. As the buyer, you would not be able to use the extra 1% towards your down payment.

Now the seller can only pay the actual closing costs, up to 6%. That means if your closing costs are only 5% the seller wouldn't be able to contribute 6% just so you could use the extra 1% towards your down payment.

This is why it's so important for you to work with a real estate agent that understands how to structure a deal to maximize the amount of money available to cover your down payment and closing costs.

Why would a seller be willing to pay my Closing Costs?

Not all sellers will want to do this. But for the right situation, it's a great tool to help sell their property fast.

For example, if my client is a qualified buyer, they are pre-approved with the mortgage company and have their down payment is covered through savings or alternative funding source but they are just short on cash, then it might make sense for a seller to agree to pay buyer closing costs rather than let their house sit on the market waiting for another buyer.

This is also why I'm so diligent when calculating what my client's closing costs are going to be. Having accurate numbers allows me the best chance to negotiate a deal with the seller that will minimize the amount of money you need to take out of your own pocket.

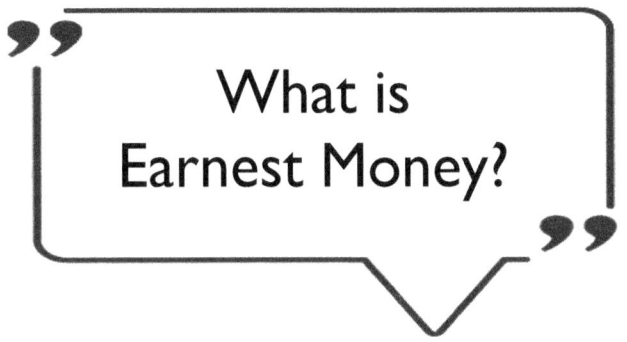

What is Earnest Money?

Earnest money may sound like it's the same as a down payment, but it's not, it's a deposit the buyer makes to the real estate broker or title company once the seller agrees to the purchase offer.

The amount of Earnest money you need is negotiable, but 2% a general rule of thumb. It lets the seller know you are serious enough about buying the house for them to take it off the market. Once the seller accepts your offer by returning a signed agreement of sale, you will generally need to have this deposit the required party with 1-5 days.

2% of a $200,000 purchase means you would need to write an earnest money check for

$4,000. Depending on how the deal is structured, between down payment assistance, gifted funds and/or seller contributions that are available, it's possible to get the amount of that Earnest Money deposit back at closing, still making it a No Money Down deal.

> **Are there any other upfront costs?**

There are a few other costs associated with purchasing your house that can often be paid at closing out of the available funds.

However, sometimes you may be required to pay for them upfront prior to closing. In that case, you can often recover those costs from the available down payment assistance, gifted funds or seller contributions, similarly to Earnest Money.

Appraisal Fees

All lenders require appraisals. They protect both you and the lender by having a professional appraiser verify the true market value of the property.

In most cases, you're going to have to pay for your lender to order an appraisal on the house in advance. Sometimes that cost is included in a mortgage application fee. A general rule of thumb for appraisal costs is $350 to $550.

Homeowners Insurance

A lot of people don't realize that homeowner's insurance is not typically required to be paid prior to settlement.

However, many insurance agents will request that it be paid as soon as they provide you a quote. I always advise my clients to request that the quoted invoice be sent to the Title company to be paid at closing rather than paying for it upfront.

Inspection Fees

Having a professional inspection done on the physical condition of a house is extremely important. I make sure that an acceptable inspection report is included in my client's contract as a condition of closing the sale.

Home inspection companies always require payment in advance. Costs for a basic home inspection are typically $350-$550.

Additional fees may be added to include a thorough pest and/or septic inspections.

PA NO MONEY DOWN HOMES

267-217-2856

PANoMoneyDownHomes.com

PA License # RS3379

> **Will I get the upfront payments back if the deal falls through?**

Earnest money is generally refundable if the deal falls through for a legitimate reason and the buyer is not in breach of contract terms.

Fees like Title Insurance, Taxes and Insurance won't be paid unless the deal closes.

Upfront costs like appraisal and inspection fees that are paid in advance for services rendered and are not refundable if the deal falls. You will lose that money.

Because appraisal and inspection requirements vary based on the type of financing being used, it is important that your real estate agent understands the loan program and the property condition requirements associated with that loan.

I'm going to make sure we know as much information about the condition of that house BEFORE you commit to spending money on an appraisal or inspections. Because I know that's money you can't get back.

> **Can you share an example of how you help overcome these challenges?**

I had a customer last year that found me through Facebook. He and his wife came to my office to talk with me about the possibilities of buying a home.

Because they had limited funds to work with, they didn't believe home ownership was within reach.

At one point, he looked me in the eye and said, "It's now or never. If I can't do it now, I'm giving up."

I really found that interesting and told him there's no reason for it not to happen if the information he had given me was accurate.

We put him and his wife in touch with a lender who was able to get them pre-approved.

The primary mortgage approval was through USDA, and the other mortgage was through PHFA, is a down payment assistance program that allowed them to finance up to $6000 of the closing costs involved in the purchase.

With the pre-approval in hand, we started our search for a home to fit their needs and their lifestyle. In a few short weeks, we found a great home.

The original sale price was $215,000 but that had just been reduced to $205,000 because the buyer had already entered an agreement to purchase a new home.

Based on comparable sales, I was convinced the home would appraise for $211,000 and we would be able to offer that number as the sale price and ask for the $6000 difference as a seller assist.

The net result to the buyer was that they were able to complete that purchase for a total of $105 out of pocket.

PA NO MONEY DOWN HOMES

SETTLEMENT SHEET BREAKDOWN

Buyer's Estimated Closing Cost

Buyer:		Settlement Date:	3/29/2019
Property:		Purchase Price:	$225,000.00
Township / Borough:		Down Payment (.000%):	$0.00
County:		Mortgage Amount:	$225,000.00
Loan:		MIP Financed:	$2,250.00
Interest Rate:	4.5%		

CLOSING COSTS

Mortgage Origination Fee (.444%):	$1,000.00	Transfer Tax (1.000%):	$2,250.00
Mortgage Discount Points (.000%):	$0.00	Deed Recording Fee:	$195.00
Appraisal:	$450.00	Mortgage Recording Fee:	$175.00
Mortgage Insurance:	$2,250.00	Notary Fee:	$45.00
Flood Certification:	$0.00	Homeowners Insurance:	$800.00
Courier:	$0.00	Home Inspection (POC):	$450.00
Wire:	$0.00	Termite / Pest Inspection (POC):	$105.00
Escrow Waiver:	$0.00	Radon Inspection (POC):	$150.00
Mortgage Interest to end of month (3) days):	$83.22	Water Inspection (POC):	$0.00
		Septic Inspection (POC):	$0.00
Mortgage Origination Costs:	**$3,783.22**	Endorsements to title:	$230.00
		Closing Protection Letter:	$125.00
Title Insurance Policy (Enhanced Sale):	$1,854.35	**Other Closing Costs:**	**$4,475.00**
Survey:	$0.00		
Title Insurance Costs:	**$1,854.35**		
Total Closing Costs:			**$10,112.57**

ESCROWS

County Tax (3 months):	$107.57		
Municipal Tax (3 months):	$106.59		
School Tax (9 months):	$1,785.25		
Homeowners Insurance (2 months):	$133.33		
Condo / HOA Fee (0 months):	$0.00		
Mortgage Insurance (2 months):	$131.24		
Total Escrows:	**$2,262.98**		

BUYER REIMBURSMENTS TO SELLER

County Tax (9 months 3 days):	$327.73
Municipal Tax (9 months 3 days):	$321.70
School Tax (3 months 2 days):	$613.02
Condo / HOA Fee (0 months 3 days):	$0.00
Total Reimbursements to Seller:	**$1,262.45**

TRANSACTION SUMMARY

Purchase Price:	$225,000.00
Closing Costs:	$10,112.57
Lender Escrows:	$2,262.98
Reimbursements to Seller:	$1,262.45
Total Acquisition Costs:	**$238,638.00**
Mortgage Amount:	($225,000.00)
MIP Financed:	($2,250.00)
Total Mortgage Amount:	**($227,250.00)**
Seller Assist (4.444%):	($10,000.00)
Estimated Cash Needed to Purchase:	**$1,388.00**
Earnest Deposit:	($0.00)
Prepaid Services:	($715.00)
Estimated Cash Needed at Settlement:	**$673.00**

ONGOING MONTHLY PAYMENTS

Principal and Interest:	$1,151.44
Real Estate Taxes:	$269.42
Homeowners Insurance:	$66.67
Mortgage Insurance:	$65.62
Condo / HOA Fee:	$0.00
Estimated Monthly Payment:	**$1,553.15**

Notice to Buyer: Buyer is encouraged to obtain an owner's title insurance policy to protect the Buyer. An owner's title insurance policy is different from a lender's insurance policy, which will not protect the Buyer from claims and attacks on the title. Owner's title insurance policies come in standard and enhanced versions; the Buyer should consult with a title insurance agent about Buyer's options.

The above figures are estimated settlement costs only. These will be adjusted as of the date of the final settlement, if necessary. The estimated monthly payment may be higher or lower because of the mortgage interest rate, type of loan and/or length of term. Buyer should consult the mortgage lender regarding exact mortgage costs and terms. I (we) acknowledge receipt of a copy of this information.

Buyer: _____ Buyer: _____

Date: _____ Date: _____

ASK TIM DIMMICK

CLOSING COSTS

(1)
Mortgage Origination Fee : (.444%) :	$1,000.00
Mortgage Discount Points (.000%):	$0.00
Appraisal: :	$450.00
Mortgage Insurance:	$2,250.00
Flood Certification:	$0.00
Courier:	$0.00
Wire:	$0.00
Escrow Waiver:	$0.00
Mortgage Interest to end of month (3) days):	$83.22
Mortgage Origination Costs:	**$3,783.22**

(2)
Title Insurance Policy (Enhanced Sale):	$1,854.35
Survey:	$0.00
Title Insurance Costs:	**$1,854.35**

(3)
Settlement Date:	3/29/2019
Purchase Price:	$225,000.00
Down Payment (.000%) :	$0.00
Mortgage Amount:	$225,000.00
MIP Financed:	$2,250.00

(4)
Transfer Tax (1.000%):	$2,250.00
Deed Recording Fee:	$165.00
Mortgage Recording Fee:	$175.00
Notary Fee:	$45.00
Homeowners Insurance:	$800.00
Home Inspection (POC) :	$450.00
Termite / Pest Inspection (POC) :	$105.00
Radon Inspection: (POC) :	$160.00
Water Inspection (POC) :	$0.00
Septic Inspection (POC) :	$0.00
Endorsements to title :	$200.00
Closing Protection Letter :	$125.00
Other Closing Costs:	**$4,475.00**

Total Closing Costs:	**$10,112.57**

Here you see a breakdown of closing costs that the buyer is typically responsible for on a home with a $225,000 purchase price.

Section 1 details the fees charged by the lender, including, Appraisal and PMI (Private Mortgage Insurance).

Section 2 details the Title Insurance cost.

Section 3 details the Settlement Date and the total amount being financed by the mortgage company.

Section 4 details the amount of taxes, insurance, inspection fees, and other miscellaneous fees charged to the borrower.

The total comes out to $10,112. 57, which is around 5% of the purchase price of the house.

*(POC) stands for "Paid Outside of Closing," meaning the borrower paid these closing costs prior to settlement.

ASK TIM DIMMICK

5 ESCROWS

County Tax (3 months):	$107.57
Municipal Tax (3 months):	$105.59
School Tax (9 months):	$1,785.25
Homeowners Insurance (2 months):	$133.33
Condo / HOA Fee (0 months):	$0.00
Mortgage Insurance (2 months):	$131.24
Total Escrows:	**$2,262.98**

6 BUYER REIMBURSMENTS TO SELLER

County Tax (9 months 3 days):	$327.73
Municipal Tax (9 months 3 days):	$321.70
School Tax (3 months 2 days):	$613.02
Condo / HOA Fee (0 months 3 days):	$0.00
Total Reimbursements to Seller:	**$1,262.45**

7 TRANSACTION SUMMARY

Purchase Price:	$225,000.00
Closing Costs:	$10,112.57
Lender Escrows:	$2,262.98
Reimbursements to Seller:	$1,262.45
Total Acquisition Costs:	**$238,638.00**
Mortgage Amount:	($225,000.00)
MIP Financed:	($2,250.00)
Total Mortgage Amount:	**($227,250.00)**
Seller Assist (4.444%) :	($10,000.00)
Estimated Cash Needed to Purchase:	**$1,388.00**
Earnest Deposit:	($0.00)
Prepaid Services:	($715.00)
Estimated Cash Needed at Settlement:	**$673.00**

Section 5 details the amount of money the lender is holding back in an escrow account to make future taxes and insurance payments on behalf of the borrower.

Section 6 details the amount of money the buyer is reimbursing the seller for the current year's taxes already paid by the seller.

Section 7 is a summary of the transaction. Notice that the seller is contributing $10,000 towards the buyer's closing costs.

As you can see from the bottom line, this buyer only needed a total of $1388.00 out of pocket to close on the purchase of this $225,000 home.

> **Should I get approved for a loan before I start house shopping?**

The biggest mistake I see many first-time homebuyers make is they don't take the time to meet with a professional in advance about their financing options and get a game plan together so that when they think they are ready to buy they actually are.

When people come to me, they're excited about buying a house, but often haven't considered what it takes to get approved for a loan. The first thing I tell them to do is to get pre-approved.

PA NO MONEY DOWN HOMES

Sometimes they're scared about the pre-approval process because they've never been through it.

They don't know what's involved, or if it's going to cost them money. However, what's most important is it will educate them on what to do and what not to do with their credit profile while they are preparing to buy a home.

Too many times we see people try to get approved 30 days after taking out a new car loan that should have been avoided but wasn't because they were unaware as to how it would affect their qualifying.

Pre-approvals are almost a mandatory thing now. Sellers aren't going to accept an offer or take their house off the market without knowing that your loan is pre-approved.

You will never win a bid on a property without a pre-approval when you're competing with another offer with a buyer who has been pre-approved.

Your agent should be doing their homework and help you understand why this is an important step that needs to take place before looking at properties that you get excited about but may not even qualify for. This doesn't do you or your agent any good.

How do you avoid these mistakes? First and foremost, get additional advice from a professional that has helped others take the step into home ownership for the first time.

This means not only an experienced real estate agent but also a loan originator representing a reputable lender that you can sit with and look at eye to eye and know they have your best interests at heart.

Second, quit worrying about artificial things, and buy a house that fits your lifestyle and is within your means.

PA NO MONEY DOWN HOMES

There is more to living than just making a mortgage payment. There will be plenty of opportunities to move up to a larger home in years to come if you do things right the first time.

> What's the difference between Pre-Qualification and Pre-Approval?

A Pre-Qualification is issued by a mortgage originator based on the information you provide in a 10 to 15-minute phone conversation or perhaps an online application.

This will help give you a rough idea of the amount of loan you may qualify for.

A Pre-Approval is issued once the loan originators have reviewed and verified your pertinent documentation, like pay stubs, tax returns, and bank statements, along with reviewing your credit report.

PA NO MONEY DOWN HOMES

267-217-2856

PANoMoneyDownHomes.com

PA License # RS337966

> **What are the main things lenders are looking at when pre-approving a buyer?**

The three main categories that lenders look at during the pre-approval process are income, assets, and credit profile.

Income

Lenders want to see that your income is predictable and stable.

Hourly or salaried full-time employees are easier for lenders to evaluate than someone with part-time wages or who are paid on a commission and/or bonus basis. With variable income, lenders will typically average the income history for the past 24 months.

What if you're self-employed? That can be a bit more of a challenge, but not one we can't overcome. Again, the lenders are looking for a 24-month history. Let's say you worked as an employee tinting windows at a car wash for a couple of years then you decided to venture out and start your own window tinting business.

When applying for pre-approval, you would have one full year of verified income. For the year you were self-employed, your income would be verified with your tax returns. It's very important to understand that it's not based on the gross receipts from your business. Expenses must be subtracted, and you can only claim the income based on the amount of money you paid taxes on.

Ask Tim Dimmick

Assets

You must be able to provide a complete paper trail of where all the money that's being used to complete the transaction is coming from, and there can't be any loopholes. You can't withdraw money from one bank account and six weeks later deposit it into another account. That's not an easy paper trail to the source.

Mortgage lenders want to know that these funds are not borrowed in any manner that is not accounted for on your loan application. You must be able to document all funds and deposits being used for a minimum of 60 days prior to closing.

Gifted funds are very common and acceptable on most mortgage programs if they are from a family member or somebody with whom you have a long-standing relationship.

It's recommended that gifted funds either be deposited into the buyer's bank account a minimum of two weeks prior to closing or given directly to the title company from the gift donor. Either way, you have to show proof of where it's coming from.

Credit

Credit scores are used as an indication of the overall level of risk associated with lending money to any particular person. The higher the credit score, the lower the risk factor to the lender making the loan. Being a low-risk borrower typically means you can qualify for a lower interest rate.

A low credit score is associated with a higher risk for a borrower to default on the loan. So, to offset that risk, lenders will typically charge a higher interest rate on that loan.

The better your credit score, the more options you have.

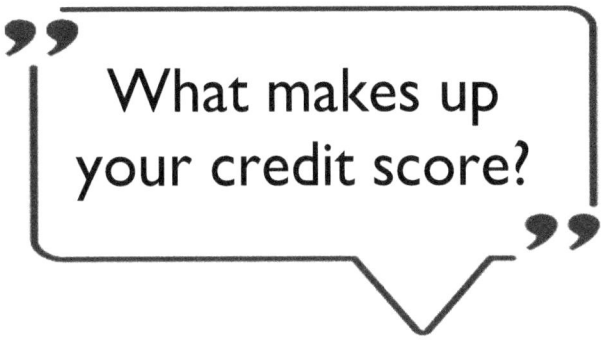

What makes up your credit score?

There are five factors that go into an overall credit score.

Payment History - This is the most influential factor. It represents how dependable you are in making timely payments. While one or two late payments in the past won't ruin your credit score, it can have a negative impact. But completely missing payments or non-payments and delinquencies can have a long-term impact on your score that can only be healed over time by establishing consistent payments and habits with the accounts you still have available.

Account Balances - Represents the percentage of your available credit limit that you have outstanding with each creditor. This is the next most influential factor.

Statistically, if somebody maxes out all of the credit on their credit cards, it's an indicator of financial distress and possible unwillingness or inability to save or manage money.

Of course, there are exceptions. People sometimes experience difficult circumstances where they may have been out of work for some time and had to live on credit cards.

People in these types of situations can benefit from working with a mortgage professional who understands the factors that make up a credit score. They can analyze your situation, identify how much you need to pay down on the right accounts that will have the biggest impact on raising your score the fastest.

Types of Credit - Represents different types of installment and revolving accounts you have used (credit cards, student loans, auto loans, etc.).

Installment loans are weighted differently than revolving credit. Installment debt is a fixed repayment type loan.

The lender gives you a certain amount of money and you repay the loan in regular (generally monthly) payments over a fixed amount of time until the loan and any interest has been paid off.

Mortgages, car loans, and student loans are examples of installment debt. This debt cannot be re-established without a new account being established.

Revolving credit is when a creditor gives you a predetermined limit of money that you can borrow as you need it.

The amount of your monthly payments depends on how much of the credit limit you have outstanding.

Credit cards are the most common type of revolving credit.

Outstanding balances can fluctuate significantly with revolving credit. If your outstanding balance reaches 50% to 75% of the limit, you will likely see a decline in your credit score very quickly.

But the good news is that as soon as you pay down that outstanding balance below the 50% level, your scores will go right back up just as quickly.

However, if you miss payments on an installment debt, like an auto loan or student loan, it can affect your credit score much longer, and the only thing that's going to help fix that is time,

New Credit - Represents accounts you've recently opened and credit inquiries from accounts you've applied for.

Opening or even just applying for several credit cards within a short period of time will cause multiple inquiries to appear on your credit report. This can be interpreted as a higher risk and may lower your score.

However, multiple inquiries within a 30-day time frame for a mortgage, car, or student loans are typically treated as a single inquiry and will typically have little to no impact on your credit score after the first inquiry.

Length of Credit History - Represents the length of time you've established and used credit accounts.

The longer you've had open credit accounts in good standing, the more positive impact it can have on your credit score.

A common mistake people make is thinking that closing revolving accounts will improve their credit score. But this can actually hurt your score.

When the account is removed from your credit report, especially if it is one of your older accounts, it shortens the length of your credit history. It also can raise the percentage of credit you have outstanding versus the amount of credit you have available.

Typically, open debt with no or low limits shows a person is able to manage their debt and results in higher scores.

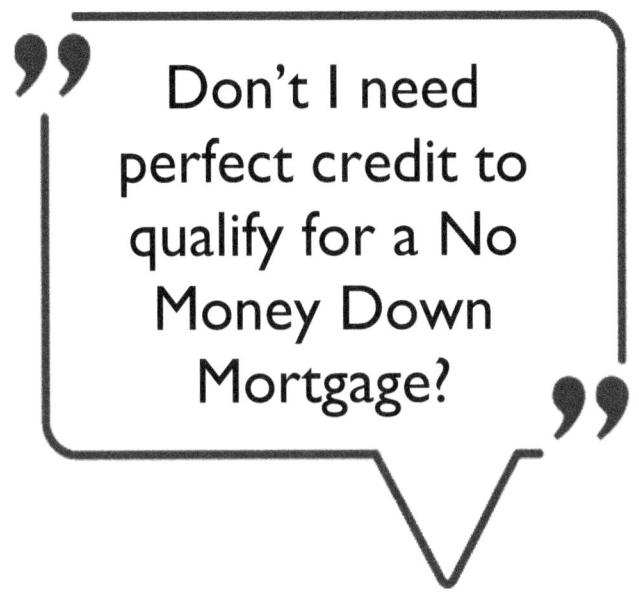

> Don't I need perfect credit to qualify for a No Money Down Mortgage?

One of the biggest misconceptions people have about qualifying for a No Down Payment home loan.

Considering a lender is loaning you 100% of the purchase price on the home, it's natural to think that one's credit would have to be stellar and would require a score over 700 or more.

This is far from the truth as lenders can approve these loans with scores in the range of

640 as long as the other qualifications are met. Each financing program has its own guideline for allowable credit scores.

One's credit scores are provided by each credit bureau and are derived from past credit payment history, the number of trade lines on your report, balances vs limits on outstanding debt, as well as other factors.

If the buyer's credit scores do not fall into line with the program requirements, we can provide the necessary guidance needed to get the scores in line for qualification.

The best advice I can give anyone that is concerned about their credit situation is to provide themselves with enough time to get the credit items worked out.

Meeting with a qualified loan originator in advance is the key.

> **Will I have to pay a higher interest rate for a No Money Down Mortgage?**

Most people believe they will pay a much higher interest rate on the loan as well as a much higher Mortgage Insurance premium.

Neither of those is accurate.

Since these loans are backed and insured by government agencies, they typically carry an interest rate that is good as a conventional loan requiring 5, 10, or even 20% down.

As far as the mortgage insurance that is required on the loan, this rate is cheaper on a USDA loan with 100% financing compared to an FHA loan that requires 3.5% down.

> **Can I qualify for a No Money Down Mortgage if I already have monthly car payments and other bills?**

Yes, you can.

Debt Ratios are one of the factors lenders use to determine how much of a mortgage you can qualify for.

There are two debt ratios that lenders will evaluate, the first being the Housing Payment ratio, and the second being Total Debt Payment Ratio. The housing payment ratio is calculated by taking the proposed house payment divided into your gross allowable or qualifying income.

The second ratio known as the Total Debt Payment Ratio will be calculated by adding any current monthly debt payments to the proposed housing payment and dividing that number into your gross monthly qualifying income.

If these ratios do not fall into the allowable program guidelines the buyer will have to either pay down their current debt load or buy a lower priced home to bring these ratios into the allowable limits for the program they are using to finance.

How Much Can I Be Approved For?

Loan programs use a debt-to-income ratio to calculate how much money a homebuyer is qualified to borrow based on the monthly payments, their income, and current credit obligations.

Calculating your debt-to-income ratio isn't as complicated as it might sound. It's really just simple division – a top number and a bottom number.

To calculate your current debt-to-income ratio, add up all your outstanding monthly credit obligations (student loans, car loans, minimum credit card payments) and divide them by your gross monthly income (the amount of income you earn before taking out any taxes and other deductions).

For example, if you make $10,000 a month in gross income and your monthly car payments, minimum credit card payments and student loan payments add up to $2500, you would calculate your current debt-to-income ratio like this:

$$\$2{,}500 \div \$10{,}000 = .25$$

So, your current debt to income ratio would be 25%.

Keep in mind your outstanding credit obligations do not include things like living expenses (current rent payments, cable, utilities, health insurance).

Most loan programs allow for a maximum **Total Debt-to-Income Ratio** of 45%.

Given the previous calculation, this means your current outstanding monthly credit obligations **along with your projected new mortgage payment** cannot exceed 45% of your monthly gross income.

$10,000 x .45 = $4,500

Since your current outstanding monthly credit obligations add up to $2,500, you would potentially qualify for up to a $2,000 monthly mortgage payment.

Your total Debt-To-Income Ratio takes into consideration all your current outstanding monthly credit obligations along with your projected new mortgage payment divided by your monthly gross income.

While 45% is typically the maximum Total Debt-To-Income Ratio allowed, there are some loan programs, such as FHA, that may approve up to 50%.

One of the biggest reasons and benefits of being pre-approved is so you can know exactly what type of loan program you qualify for and how much you will be able to borrow before you start shopping for a house.

Your real estate agent should be able to help you estimate your payment based on the loan program, the home purchase price plus the taxes and homeowner's insurance along with any association fees if applicable.

> **I just got a new job. Can I still qualify for a No Money Down Mortgage?**

That's another big misconception. People think they need to have held the same job for at least two years.

Your lender is looking for consistency and advancement in your employment more than the length of employment. They don't want to see you going backward or going from a W2 employee to a self-employed person without a track record.

They don't want to see you change fields while stepping down in income in any way.

If you're in the same line of work, they won't necessarily care if you've had two or three jobs in the last two years, as long as it's in the same line of work and you've bettered yourself along the way.

That's a positive thing, and a lender is not going to hold that against you. However, when you have employment gaps, change your field of work, have big income swings, or decide to go work on your own without a track record can cause an underwriter to bulk at approving your loan.

> **Are there any pitfalls I should look out for?**

The biggest pitfalls I see from first-time buyers is that they often want to allow their emotions and excitement, override fundamentally sound decisions.

I tell a lot of my clients that I try to be the voice of reason during the purchase and advise them on what's in their best interest and will serve them well after the initial excitement diminishes.

I don't want them to overlook or even consider settling for something that isn't right when it is the responsibility of the seller just because they are afraid of losing the deal.

These are the decisions they will regret 30, 60 and 90 days after the purchase. I remind them they won't be able to pick up the phone and call their landlord.

First-time buyers also tend to stretch what they conceive to be affordable and in their price range.

While the lender may approve them for a larger loan, it doesn't mean they will be comfortable making the increased payment.

So, in these situations, I encourage them to try to save that extra money each month. If they can do it comfortably and it isn't a burden, then go for it.

> **How much do real estate agents charge to help me through the process of finding the right house?**

Good news. As the buyer, it doesn't cost you anything. In the state of Pennsylvania, the seller pays all the real estate agent fees as a commission based on a percentage of the sales price of the house. That commission is typically split equally between the listing agent, the person that does the marketing for the house and the agent who is representing the buyer.

So, unlike hiring most consultants or service providers from insurance agents, accounts, or even chiropractors, cost isn't really a consideration.

This is why you should really do your homework and find an agent that understands your situation and is going to work hard to help you fulfill your dream of owning a home. Because for the buyer, a great agent costs just as much as a bad agent. In fact, a bad agent will most likely cost you more in the long run.

> **What inspired you to help people buy their first home with no money down?**

Prior to entering the real estate field, I ran my own mortgage brokerage for 21 years.

During this time, I became very familiar with the products that existed to help first-time buyers get into a home with limited cash but had very limited exposure to both realtors and home buyers.

After the real estate crash that took place from 2008-2010, many people believed that these types of loans were a large contributing factor for the crash.

What is ironic is these loans had a lower foreclosure and delinquency rate than most. Also, these loans remained through-out the crisis and continue to be a great choice still available to first-time homebuyers today.

So, from my experience in the home mortgage finance business, I knew that most buyers and many realtors were unaware or did not understand the many financing options that existed to make a home purchase possible with limited funds.

In today's market of rising real estate prices, and interest rates it is difficult for many to save money at a pace to offset the impact these two items have on one's proposed mortgage payment.

My passion is fueled by watching individuals and couples who are starting out paying monthly rents of $1200-$1700 a month when they could own a home with a comparable payment.

Most individuals would choose to own if they are shown how they can accomplish it.

Many buyers are skeptical at first, and while not saying it out loud, inside are saying "prove it to me." To those, I say as long as you are willing to follow the advice and direction provided I will prove to you that home ownership is within your reach.

I'm more interested in finding buyers the right opportunity, not the first opportunity.

When someone comes to me with very limited funds, they have to be prepared to lose out on a few offers along the way.

Every situation is different; every seller is in a different position in their life and may or may not be willing to give the buyer a seller assist. The property may or may not be valued higher than the sale price, limiting the ability to finance in some of the closing costs.

Market conditions also play a major factor, as in a seller's market it becomes more difficult because of more buyers than sellers vs. a buyer's market when there are more sellers than buyers.

So, it is important for each buyer to fully understand their situation, the current market conditions and what needs to take place to make a successful transaction happen.

> **What big lesson have you learned from working with first-time homebuyers?**

The biggest lesson I've learned is to be very thorough throughout the whole process.

There are many moving parts to each transaction, and most are items that a first-time buyer is unaware of because it is their first experience buying a home.

That being said, the number one thing I pay attention to is the condition of the home and its major components. I do not want a buyer with limited funds to even think of buying a home that appears to be uncared for and in disrepair.

The first problem that can arise from this situation would be my buyer spending money on inspections that reveal issues that will cause the deal to not close and wasting precious limited funds that they cannot recoup.

When you walk into a home and it's not clean or taken care of, it's often a sign they haven't taken care of routine maintenance of major components either.

While the price may be attractive because of the condition, it will not be a property that a first-time buyer will be happy with if they move in and do not have the money to make repairs.

> What's the most important question a first-time home buyer should ask themselves before buying a home with no money down?

The most important thing they should ask themselves is "Can I afford it?"

They need to be comfortable making that proposed monthly payment because there are many additional items such as property maintenance and improvements that come along with home ownership. Items that they may not be paying attention to if they are currently in a rental.

The last thing I want to happen is to run into my clients a year later to hear that they have regrets. Instead, I want them to be thrilled that they made the decision to be a homeowner and love their home.

A great way for a buyer to know they are making the right decision is for them to pretend they have that payment before they do.

If the price range of the home you want to buy is going to result in a $1600 mortgage payment, and you are currently only paying $1300 in rent, for the next 90 days, save that $300 difference.

This will allow you to see the impact the mortgage will have on your budget.

> What is the most important thing a first-time home buyer should consider when evaluating a real estate agent?

In my opinion, when choosing a realtor look for one that has a great reputation in serving their clients.

There are many sources to view reviews online. Sites such as Realtor.com and Zillow offer a great source for viewing reviews.

Also, choose a realtor that spends a lot of time working with first-time homebuyers.

These agents will typically have a better understanding of finance options available to first-time homebuyers, and should also have a better understanding of how to structure an offer to coincide with your circumstances.

How do I get this process started?

The best way to get the pre-approval process rolling is to schedule a meeting with me so we can talk about your situation.

I'll put you in touch with a mortgage lender that specializes in working with first-time home buyer loan programs and can determine which best fit your needs.

Be prepared to provide the mortgage company with two of your most recent pay stubs, two of your most recent bank statements, and the two most recent years of filed tax returns and W2s.

You'll be in the hands of professionals who know the ins and outs of the mortgage business and can analyze your documents quickly.

In as little as 24 hours, we should know what kind of program you qualify for and how much house you can afford. That's when the fun begins.

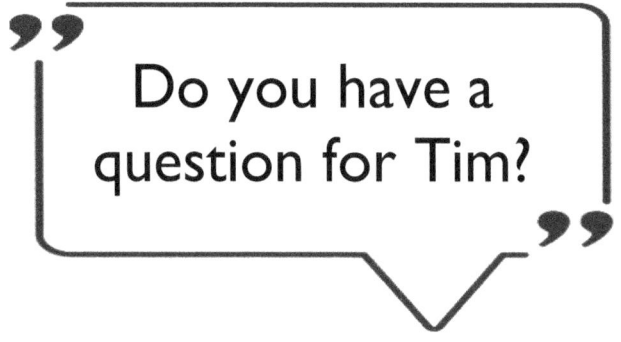

Do you have a question for Tim?

If you have more questions about buying a home with No Money Down, then let me know. I'm happy to talk with you and help you to evaluate your unique situation.

Phone

267-217-2856

Email

timdimmick@remax.net

Website

PANoMoneyDownHomes.com

Facebook

Facebook.com/PANoMoneyDownHomes

PA NO MONEY DOWN HOMES

267-217-2856

PANoMoneyDownHomes.com

PA License # RS337966

About Tim Dimmick

With a combined 24 years' experience in the Home Finance and Real Estate fields, Tim offers superior service to clients wishing to buy and sell residential real estate in the Bucks, Montgomery, Lehigh and Berks County areas of Pennsylvania. Buying and selling a home is often a very emotional experience, and Tim is the voice of reason to his customers, keeping reality within focus throughout the process.

As a buyer's representative, Tim's number one goal is to find you a home that meets your needs, your lifestyle and is within your budget. While everyone would like the next bigger home with more bells and whistles, the reality is you will be happiest in a home that is geographically located in an area that your life is built around and is priced for your income level. Owning a home is very enjoyable; however, there is more to life than making a mortgage payment.

Tim has a great understanding of loan programs, and how to structure your offer to match up with your current financial situation and long-term goals. Whether it is your first or tenth time buying a home, Tim will do his best to make your home buying process an enjoyable experience.

If you or anyone you know is looking to buy a home in the areas that Tim services, he would welcome the opportunity to earn their business!

What Tim's Clients Are Saying

- DB Koenig

"Tim was fantastic to work with through the whole process, start to finish. I was very particular with what I wanted, and he never got frustrated with me. He was very knowledgeable about the financing process as well as what to look for within the homes. We couldn't have asked for anyone better! We would definitely recommend him and will use him again if we decide to ever purchase another home!!!"

- Tim & Kim O.

"I highly recommend Timothy Dimmick. He's very proactive. He got us appointments to see places we asked about almost immediately. We worked with him over a period of a week and found the place we wanted. I would text him about a place I saw and we basically had a showing that day. Sometimes several in one day. Which I loved because that's what I wanted.

He was light and friendly during our stresses which helped me a lot. I would try to jump on a place because I'm an anxious person and he kept me calm instead to allow a proper decision to be made. We closed on a place yesterday, and I couldn't be happier with the outcome. In my opinion, I would highly recommend him to anyone."

- Chrissy L.

Tim Dimmick made our dreams come true. We met with Tim in early October and got moved into our new home the end of December. Tim made himself available around our crazy schedules. Tim makes you feel like family and not business. I am already spreading his name around town. Tim is very professional and took time to answer all of our questions and concerns. This was our first home buying, and he made the experience so smooth and easy. I would highly recommend Tim to family, friends, coworkers and just meeting people. If you're looking for your new home, go to Tim he knows the business very well. Thank you, Tim for everything I appreciate you and your support.

- Amanda H.

"We can't recommend Tim enough!! Tim not only has extensive knowledge of the real estate market, but he also has extensive knowledge of every kind of mortgage loan. We were first time home buyers and went into this process with limited knowledge of how everything worked. I cannot stress enough how ABOVE and BEYOND Tim went to make us feel comfortable with the entire process from start to finish. He truly makes you feel like you are his only client, calling us often just to check in, and taking his time to answer all of our questions, and give us his recommendations. He makes himself available whenever we needed him. We would recommend Tim over and over a million times!!! It doesn't get better than him!".

- Sarah B.

"My husband and I had a wonderful experience working with Tim! He knew what we were looking for and he worked hard to help us find our perfect home. He was very timely with all of the paperwork and very professional.

We learned quickly that we could trust him to find us our new home and he did what he could to find all the information needed for any home we were interested in to let us know if it would be a good fit for what we needed. We have already recommended him to friends pursuing their new homes! I believe I can speak for the both of us when I say that we highly recommend Tim when it comes to your buying or selling needs!"

www.ingramcontent.com/pod-product-compliance
Lightning Source LLC
Chambersburg PA
CBHW072217170526
45158CB00002BA/641